Hunting Prey

By Clem King

Contents

Hunting

Some animals eat other animals.

They hunt these animals.

The animals they hunt are called “prey”.

Big Cats

Big cats hunt prey on flat land called plains.

They wait for prey.
Then they chase the prey.

If the big cats fail to get the prey, they will be hungry.

They have no time for breaks!

Ospreys

Ospreys have big wings and strong nails.

The main prey of ospreys is fish.

Ospreys see well.

They fly up and wait to spot a fish.

Moray Eels

Moray eels look like one long tail!

They swim and sway.

Moray eels stay very still
and wait for small fish to swim by.

They dash out
and snap up the prey.

Grey Whales

Grey whales weigh a lot!

They have great big tails and brains.

Grey whales hunt krill, which are very small.

They must munch up lots of krill.

Ways of Hunting

Animals that hunt other animals have many ways to get prey.

Some animals stay still and wait.

Others are big.

And others are very quick!

CHECKING FOR MEANING

1. What do ospreys mainly eat? *(Literal)*
2. How does a moray eel catch its prey? *(Literal)*
3. Why do you think grey whales need to eat a lot? *(Inferential)*

EXTENDING VOCABULARY

prey	What does *prey* mean in this text? How is it similar to the word *food*? How is it related to the word *hunt*?
plains	The word *plains* sounds the same as the word *planes*. These words are homophones. How is the meaning of *plains* different from *planes*?
krill	Look at the word *krill*. How many sounds are in this word? Can you think of another creature that is like krill?

MOVING BEYOND THE TEXT

1. How might small fish protect themselves from ospreys and moray eels?
2. What other animals need to eat a lot, like the grey whale does?
3. What do you think an animal needs to do to be a good hunter?
4. Some animals do not eat meat or fish. What do those animals eat?

TIME TO WRITE

Write about your favourite animal in the book. You can choose a predator or a prey animal.

PRACTICE WORDS